Copyright © 2007 by Simple Truths, LLC
Published by Simple Truths, LLC 1952 McDowell Road, Suite 300, Naperville, Illinois 60563

Toll Free 800-900-3427

Cover Design: Scott Francis
Book Design: Vieceli Design Company, West Dundee, Illinois
Simple Truths is a registered trademark.
Printed and bound in the United States of America.

ISBN 978-1-60810-034-7

Editing by Julie Kellogg

www.simpletruths.com

09 WOZ 11

You Can't Send a Duck to Eagle School...

And Other Simple Truths of Leadership

Mac Anderson

Table of Contents

Introduction

A few years ago I had lunch with a top executive from a company known for their legendary retail service. My wife and I are both huge fans, and over lunch I shared with him some of the great service stories his people had provided the Anderson family. I said, "With the service your people give… you must have a training manual 2 inches thick." He looked up and said, "Mac, we don't have a training manual. What we do is find the

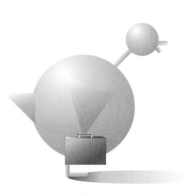

best people we can find and we empower them to do whatever it takes to satisfy the customer." Then he said something I'll never forget. He said, "We learned a long time ago that **you can't send a duck to eagle school.**" "Excuse me," I said. He repeated…**"You can't send a duck to eagle school."** He said, "You can't teach someone to smile, you can't teach someone to want to serve, you can't teach personality. What we can do, however, is hire people who have those qualities and we can then teach them about our products and teach them our culture."

As long as I live I will never forget this simple analogy about hiring people. It is branded on my brain forever. And since that day, with every hiring decision I've made, I find myself asking the question: "Am I hiring a duck thinking they will become an eagle?" I can also honestly say that asking this simple question has saved me from making some important hiring mistakes. I just wish I'd heard it 20 years sooner.

The "Duck to Eagle School" lesson is one of many "simple truths" of leadership that I've learned on my journey as an entrepreneur. In the past 30 years, I've had the good fortune to be involved with three successful start up companies, each becoming a leader in its niche. And, as you can imagine, there have been many peaks, valleys and "lessons learned" along the way. I've also been very fortunate to have met a lot of people who are a lot smarter than I. Successful entrepreneurs, authors, speakers, educators, coaches, and CEO's of large companies, have all helped shape my thinking. It has been their wisdom and their knowledge, combined with my own life experiences, that have helped shape who I am today.

My goal with this little book is to share some of my "lessons learned" in a brief, but engaging way. Because so many times, it's not what is said, but how it is said, that turns the switch from off to on. ***For me, one of the most exciting things about business and life, is that one great idea can change our life forever.***

All the Best,

Mac Anderson

Mac Anderson
Founder, Simple Truths and Successories

LEADERSHIP
WOULD BE EASY,
if it wasn't for people

There is one question that every employee will love to have you ask ... What can I do to help? So many times as leaders, we assume we're doing all we can do; however, these 6 words: **"What can I do to help?"** will usually prove your assumptions are dead wrong. The question should address three areas:

1 What can I do to help you **serve the customer** better?

2 What can I do to make your **working environment** more pleasant?

3 What can I do to help you **better balance your work** and family life?

Obviously, it's important to let them know up front that you may not be able to help with everything they ask, but you'll do what you can. In other words, a chauffer to and from work is probably out of the question.

You'll usually be amazed to hear about a few small things that will cost you next to nothing. You may find they need a new file cabinet, their chair is uncomfortable, they need flex-hours 1 day a week, a new headset for the phone, or a small space heater in the winter months. The truth is, the fact that **you've taken the time to listen** to their personal concerns is far more important in their eyes than what you'll do for them. Gallop polled over 1 million employees **who thought they had a great boss and asked them one question.** Why? You got it! The number one reason was the boss was willing to listen to what they had to say. Never forget …

it's the little things, not the big ones, that will earn the respect of your people.

"LISTENING IS WANTING TO HEAR."

— JIM CATHCART

Change Is Good...
YOU GO FIRST

About 6 months ago Tom Feltenstein said, "Mac, we should write a book together and the title could be, **Change Is Good ... You Go First.**" I immediately loved the idea and, I'm pleased to say, it is scheduled to be released soon with a subtitle of "... 21 ways to inspire change."

Change is the key that unlocks the door to growth and excitement in any organization. The leader's ability to inspire a "culture of change" can make or break their success. Tomorrow comes at us with lightning speed and our competitive advantage is a fleeting thing. Bill Gates puts it this way... "In 3 years every product my company makes will be obsolete. The only question is whether we will make it obsolete or someone else will." Peter Drucker reinforced what Gates said, by saying: **"Every 3 years, each product and process should be put on trial for its life, otherwise the competition will pass you by."** Drucker also says that most companies find it easier to come up with new ideas than to let go of old ones.

Have you ever watched a fly bouncing off a window pane, even with an open door a few feet away? Many times the fly keeps crashing into the glass until it finally dies. There are many companies in today's world doing exactly the same thing. They continue down "today's path," wearing blinders to the possibility of change.... until they die.

Keeping change and continuous improvements on the "front burner" is never easy. **We are so focused on today's problems that we put off planning for tomorrow's opportunities.**

Keeping change alive starts with rewarding **innovation, risk-taking** and **creativity**. In fact, you need to fail quickly and fail often to stay ahead of the competition. T.S. Elliot said it best, **"Only those who risk going too far can possibly find out how far to go."**

*In the end, it is important to remember
that we cannot become what we need to be
by remaining who we are."*
— MAX DEPREE

"I've spent a good part of my life *studying* economic SUCCESSES AND FAILURES… above all, I've *learned* that everything takes a back seat to *innovation*."

— TOM PETERS

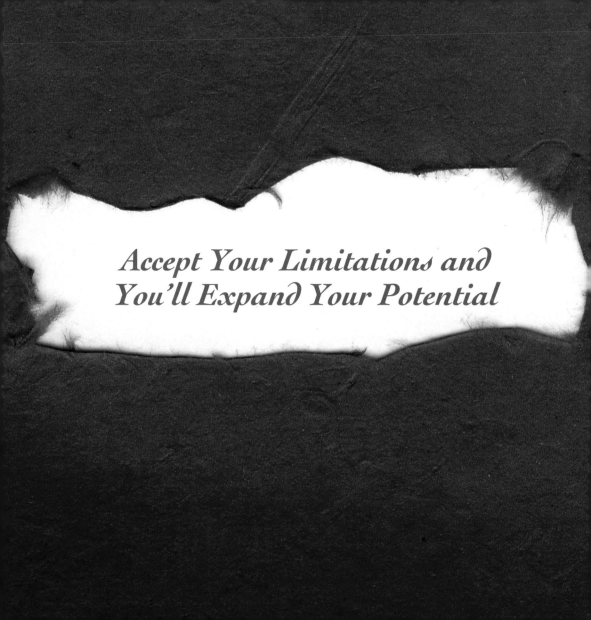

Accept Your Limitations and
You'll Expand Your Potential

One of the biggest reasons many leaders fail is their unwillingness to accept their limitations. Ego gets in the way. They feel they're smart enough to do it all, and mistakenly feel that what they don't know they can learn "on the fly." So many times it's a recipe for disaster, especially for entrepreneurs.

Walt Disney failed many times early in his career. He had brilliant ideas, but his ability to execute them was painfully lacking. He also, believe it or not, was a lousy artist. So after the third failure, **Disney was finally convinced that to succeed he must surround himself with great artists who could bring his animation ideas to life.** He also needed his brother Roy to handle the financial side of the business. These two moves made all the difference and freed Walt up to do what he did best, which was using his imagination to plan their future.

I can definitely relate to the Disney story. From 1991-93 we were on a roll at Successories. We had gone from $5 million to $45 million in three years. Then came 1994, and Murphy's Law hit us like a ton of bricks. We had grown too fast and no longer had the right people or infrastructure to handle it. Early in 1995, I realized that I had to make significant changes. After a lot of soul searching, I realized my strengths were people skills and creativity; however, my weaknesses were operations and accounting. **To grow the business and rebuild the infrastructure, I had to hire good people who had been there and done that, people who could complement what I did best.** This was a very painful wake-up call, but I learned some of the most valuable lessons of my life.

I heard a quote the other day that offers every manager and entrepreneur food for thought:

"If your company mission is to climb a tree, which would you rather do:

Hire a SQUIRREL or Train a HORSE?"

Forget REAL GOOD —
Remember FEEL GOOD

I met Tom Asacker 4 years ago at a conference in Hawaii, where we both spoke. There was one thing he said that I never forgot. He said as leaders we need to "forget real good and remember feel good."

Today, he said, there are 5 billion web pages (25 for every man, woman and child in this country) and 6 million going up every day. There are 89 brands of shampoo at Walgreens!

Customers are stressed out from information overload and conflicting information... more and more they are relying on their gut... and their feelings to make decisions.

In fact, he said, it really doesn't matter how customers feel about you and your business. What makes a difference is how your products make them feel about themselves and their decisions. Every psychologist and smart marketer knows that if a man or woman does something and it feels good, they'll do it again; if it feels bad they won't do it.

Far too many companies are focused on the product and not the experience. **We need to replace our brain with our heart** because that's often how people make decisions. Studies have proven that the essential difference between emotion and reason is that emotion leads to action and reason leads to conclusions.

What do you want? Do you want action or do you want people to think?

The question you need to ask is, "How am I making my customers feel?" Am I making them compare or care? There's a big difference. Caring and feelings drive action… the other stuff is just a tool. The bottom line is that the really hard stuff is the soft stuff…It's the feelings of your employees and customers.

That, in the end, is your competitive advantage.

"IF YOU THROW YOUR HEART OVER THE FENCE, THE REST WILL FOLLOW."

— Anonymous

ATTITUDE
isn't EVERYTHING,
but it's pretty
DARN CLOSE

When hiring someone, start with the premise that attitudes are contagious. Then ask yourself one question … *is theirs worth catching?*

I've been in business for over 30 years and I've come to realize the difference in success and failure is not how you look, not how you dress, not how much you're educated, but …

HOW YOU THINK!

In my business life, I've watched many very intelligent people fail miserably because they have a negative attitude; and, I've also observed just as many people with average intelligence soar to success because of positive attitudes.

Southwest Airlines' VP of People is often asked the question: *How do you get your people to be so nice? Her answer is always the same …*

"WE HIRE NICE PEOPLE."

It sounds almost too simple to feel important, but "hiring nice people" has been the cornerstone of their amazing success in a highly competitive industry. They understand their competitors may be able to match their price and copy their business model, however, they feel that the spirit and the attitude of their employees will be extremely difficult to replicate. Never forget …

Great customer service is only delivered
by nice, passionate, caring employees.
There is no other way it can happen.

CUSTOMER SERVICE
IS NOT A DEPARTMENT...
IT'S AN ATTITUDE.

— ANONYMOUS

THE ROAD
TO SUCCESS
IS NOT ALWAYS
A ROAD

One of my favorite books is *Paper Airplane* written by my good friend, Michael McMillan, whom I consider a creative genius … and I rarely use the "G word." Michael has the unique ability to bring simple ideas to life in an unforgettable way.

The subtitle, "A Lesson for Flying Outside the Box," is something very difficult for most leaders to do. However, history proves that creative breakthroughs in science, technology and business only occur

when people challenge the accepted norm and take action. Innovation comes from leaving the "proven" map behind to explore new territories.

In Paper Airplane, Michael shares how his sixth grade teacher, Mrs. Hackett, spent the entire week teaching the class aerodynamics. To complete the lesson, she organized a paper airplane contest. The kids were given a sheet of construction paper and 15 minutes to build the "winning" plane.

They all went to work carefully folding their paper... hoping to create a winning plane that would travel the farthest. Before long, everyone was ready to go outside to start the contest... nearly everyone. Jeff, a unique young man who marched to the beat of a different drummer, hadn't made one fold in his paper. He was staring out the window... thinking.

To give him a little more time, Mrs. Hackett told Jeff he could go last. The contest was interesting on many levels. Some of the planes barely flew five feet while others did surprisingly well. One thing was certain — the line was thinning down and Jeff was still holding a flat piece of construction paper.

Before long, Jeff was the only remaining contestant. With great anticipation, the class watched as Jeff approached with his craft well hidden behind his back. Then he stepped to the line and exposed his masterpiece… a flat sheet of paper. But as the class started to snicker, Jeff confidently wadded up the paper into a ball, and threw it farther than the leading plane had flown. **THE CROWD WENT WILD!!!**

Michael explains that Jeff demonstrated a new way of interpreting a problem and had the courage to act on his vision. He's never said, but I've always suspected Jeff's real name might be Michael.

One of my favorite quotes that hangs on my office wall is…

"You cannot discover new oceans unless you have the courage to lose sight of the shore."

A few years ago I had dinner with a friend and met his wife, Terri, for the first time. Our dinner conversation led to the fact that I had started McCord Travel and she said, "I can't believe it, I used to work for McCord." She then said, **"I have wonderful memories of my time at McCord, and I'll never forget how they treated me my first day on the job."** I sold McCord in 1985, and my friend, Bruce Black, stayed on to run the company for the new owner. So, I can take no credit for Terri's special memory.

Terri said: "There was something different happening from the moment I walked through the front door … more energy and more smiles than I was used to at other jobs. I was greeted by a very nice young lady who said that she was going to be my mentor during the first week, and if I had any questions she'd be happy to answer them. She introduced me to the people in each department. At lunch she presented me with a gift of personalized stationery. They all went the "extra mile" to make me feel at home … and, I'll never forget it."

Robert A. Baird, an employee-owned investment company from Milwaukee, was listed by Forbes Magazine as one of the 100 best companies to work for. **They believe in the personal touch.** New hires are greeted with flowers on their desk, and they also meet with the CEO for a new associates' event. The company understands that little things can make a big difference.

Another "1st Impression idea" is to send a note and a small gift to the employee's home, welcoming them on board. This way, the employee's spouse (if they're married) is left with a good first impression as well.

Most leaders grossly underestimate the power of a first impression, not only of their employees, but also, of their customers. For example, Marj Webber was my assistant at Successories. Among other duties, Marj was responsible for dealing with the various photography companies that we used for our prints, cards, etc. One day she came into my office and said, **"I've been doing this for a long time, but this is the nicest letter I've ever received."** She said she had just placed an order with Alaska Stock Images and received this letter a few days later. Here's what it said:

Dear Marjorie,

Thank you for your recent purchase. We appreciate the opportunity to serve you and look forward to working with you again. We hope you'll enjoy the enclosed gift.

Satisfied customers are our best advertisement, so I encourage you to give us feedback on how we're doing. If we ever disappoint you, I hope you'll let us know; we'll do everything we can to make things right.

In the meantime, if you have any questions or require assistance, please feel free to contact us.

Thank you again for selecting us. It is our privilege to work with you.

Sincerely,
Laurie Campbell, Alaska Stock Images

Now, you tell me...how long did it take to write this letter and send a small gift?

The answer is not long! But, the impact was powerful and lasting. It immediately separated this vendor from the competition.

Never forget, with every new employee and every new customer you have only one chance...just one, to make a great first impression. **Plan it. Make it all it can be!**

"Giving people a they expect is a back a lot more

little more than good way to get than you'd expect."

— ROBERT HALF

EAT the
FROG

There's an old saying that says… **"If the first thing you do when you wake up in the morning is eat a live frog, then nothing worse can happen for the rest of the day!"** Well, I don't know about you, but I think that's a pretty safe assumption.

Brian Tracy, in his book *Eat the Frog*, says that your **"frog"** should be the most difficult item on your things to do list, the one where you're most likely to procrastinate; because, if you eat that first, it'll give you energy and momentum for the rest of the day. But, if you don't … and let him sit there on the plate and stare at you while you do a hundred unimportant things, it can drain your energy and you won't even know it.

So, here's your assignment: for the next 30 days take a look at your list, circle the frog, and eat that first.

You'll thank me for it.

"**PROCRAS**

IS ATTITUDE'S NATURAL

SO FATIGUING AS AN

TINATION

ASSASSIN. THERE'S NOTHING UNCOMPLETED TASK."

— WILLIAM JAMES

LESS IS ALMOST ALWAYS
MORE

Two of the all-time greatest coaches in sports history were Red Auerbach, who coached the great Boston Celtics basketball team in the 1950's and 1960's, and Vince Lombardi, the legendary football coach for the Green Bay Packers. When I read their biographies, what struck me most was their **"keep it simple"** philosophy. While other coaches were teaching complicated offense and defense, both Lombardi and Auerbach only had a few plays, but this was the key … **they executed the plays to perfection.**

Someone once asked Auerbach what magic formula he had for winning games. He laughed and said, **"Our secret to success is what I would call 'effective simplicity.' Nothing complicated. In fact, we only have seven different plays, and Bill Russell touched the ball on every one of them."**

Under Auerbach's **"effective simplicity" philosophy**, the Boston Celtics won every championship from 1959 through 1966- eight years in a row, a record unmatched since.

Lombardi's coaching philosophy was strikingly similar, and he had only five running plays in his offense, but like Auerbach, executed every play to perfection. He'd often say,

"We really don't fool anyone. The opposition knows what's coming, but they rarely stop us because every player knows his assignment and we've practiced it a thousand times."

"Winning is not a some time thing, it is an all the time thing. You don't do things right once in a while... you do them right all the time."

—Vince Lombardi

Lombardi was fanatical when it came to teaching and reinforcing the basic fundamentals of the game. In his mind, blocking and tackling were the keys to winning football games. In fact, to make his point on fundamentals, every year he would begin his training camp by saying ... **"Gentlemen, this is a football."**

Get a
Second Job

You may have heard the quote ... "The speed of the leader will determine the rate of the pack." Well here's another one for you ... **"The attitude of the leader will determine the attitude of the pack."**

Because I'm the founder of Successories®, some people think that this guy probably never has a negative thought. How wrong they would be! Like every human being, **I have doubts, fears, and disappointments in my life.** As a leader, however, we must manage our attitudes. Do we need to be perfect? Of course not. But, we can never underestimate the influence that our actions and our attitudes will have on our team. Churchill said,

"The price of **LEADERSHIP** is **RESPONSIBILITY."**

...and part of that responsibility is to **STAY POSITIVE** whether you feel like it or not.

MANAGING YOUR ATTITUDE IS A VERY PERSONAL THING.

However, for me, the most important factor is exercise. My attitude and my energy levels are directly tied to exercise. I can be doing everything else right, but without regular exercise I can feel my attitude heading south.

I've got a friend who is 65 but looks like he's 55. I saw him the other day and said, "Tony, you look great." He said, "I feel great! I got a second job." I said, "A second job? I thought your import business was doing well." He said, "It is. **My second job is on the treadmill from 6-7 every morning.** When I started looking at it as a second job, I showed up whether I wanted to or not!" He said, **"The pay is lousy, but the benefits to my health and my attitude are priceless!"**

Exercise, more than anything, is a "stress buster." And, don't kid yourself, stress is a killer. In fact the World Health Organiztion estimates that **80% of all illnesses are directly or indirectly caused by stress. Therefore, if you're not proactive in busting stress, it's very likely to come back and bust you!**

CHANGE YOUR THOUGHTS AND CHANGE YOUR WORLD.

— EARL NIGHTINGALE

Wisdom is knowing
the right path to take...
INTEGRITY IS TAKING IT

The dictionary defines integrity as the state of being complete and unified. Simply put, when you have integrity, your words and your deeds match up. John Maxwell says, *"Integrity is not what we do as much as who we are. And who we are, in turn, determines what we do."* Even Socrates reminds us,

"The first key to greatness is to be in reality what we appear to be."

Integrity is never easy, but most of all requires self discipline, inner trust and honesty at all times. **The poem, "Myself," by Edgar Guest is on the next page. Keep it handy and read it often!**

"MYSELF"

I have to live with myself, and so
I want to be fit for myself to know,
I want to be able, as days go by,
Always to look myself straight in the eye;
I don't want to stand, with the setting sun,
And hate myself for things I have done.
I don't want to keep on a closet shelf
A lot of secrets about myself,
And fool myself, as I come and go,
Into thinking that nobody else will know
The kind of man I really am;

I don't want to dress up myself in sham.
I want to go out with my head erect,
I want to deserve all men's respect;
But here in the struggle for fame and pelf
I want to be able to like myself.
I don't want to look at myself and know
That I'm bluster and bluff and empty show.
I can never hide myself from me;
I see what others may never see;
I know what others might never know,
I never can fool myself, and so,
Whatever happens, I want to be
Self-respecting and conscience free.

— EDGAR GUEST

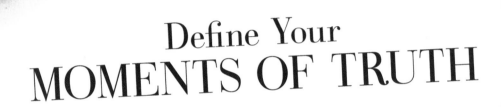
Define Your
MOMENTS OF TRUTH

In 1982, Jan Carlson had just been named the CEO of Scandinavian Airlines. His company was in trouble. They had just been ranked by a consumer poll as the worst airline in the world. Last in service, last in dependability, and last in profits as a percentage of sales. Yet one year later, in the same poll, they were ranked number one in all three categories. What happened?

Carlson had decided to focus on what he thought was the most critical issue ... serving the customer. He wanted to keep it simple:

IDENTIFY EVERY CONTACT BETWEEN THE CUSTOMER AND THE EMPLOYEE, AND TREAT THAT CONTACT AS ... "A MOMENT OF TRUTH."

He set out to let his people know the importance of that moment ... the captain, the ticket agent, the baggage handler, the flight attendant.

"EVERY MOMENT, EVERY CONTACT," HE SAID, "MUST BE AS PLEASANT, AND AS MEMORABLE AS POSSIBLE."

He figured that he had approximately ten million customers each year, and on average each customer made contact with five of his people for approximately fifteen seconds apiece. Therefore, in his mind, these fifty million contacts, fifteen seconds at a time, would determine the fate of his company.

He set out to share his vision with his twenty thousand employees. He knew the key was to empower the front line. Let them make the decision and take action, because they were Scandinavian Airlines during those fifteen seconds. He now had twenty thousand people who were energized and ready to go because they were focused on one very important thing … **making every moment count.**

"A leader's job is to look into the future and see the organization, not as it is, but as it should be."

— JACK WELCH

COMPANIES DON'T SUCCEED...
PEOPLE DO.

To build a "customer first" culture, you must put them second. Your employees must come first, because there is a rule of thumb in business that says, **"Your people will only treat your customers as well as they are being treated; thus to have satisfied customers, they must be served by passionate people."**

Howard Schultz, the founder of Starbucks, is one of my favorite leaders. His book, *Pour Your Heart Into It*, is excellent. In it he offers in great detail all the obstacles he overcame in turning his vision into reality.

Early on, Schultz realized that the key to his success was to **recruit well-educated people who were eager to communicate his passion for coffee.** This, he felt, would be his competitive advantage in an industry where turnover was 300 percent a year. To hire the best people, he also knew he must be willing to pay them more than the going wage and offer health benefits that weren't available elsewhere. He saw that part-time people made up two-thirds of his employee base, and **no one in the restaurant industry offered benefits to part-timers.**

Schultz went to work in an effort to sell his board of directors on increasing expenses while most restaurant executives in the 1980's were looking for ways to cut costs. Initially, Schultz's pleas to investors and the board fell on deaf ears because Starbucks was still losing money. But Schultz was persistent. He was looking long term and was committed to growing the business with passionate people. He won, and said many times afterwards that this decision was one of the most important decisions, if not the most important, that he made at Starbucks. **His employee retention rate was about five times the industry average**, but more importantly, he attracted people with great attitudes who made their customers feel welcome and at home.

Over the years, Schultz often showed how much he cared for his people. Early on July 7, 1997, he and his family were asleep at home in East Hampton, New York. The phone rang and he learned that three

Starbucks employees had been murdered in a botched robbery in Washington, D.C. A stunned Schultz immediately chartered a plane and arrived there before 9 a.m. that morning. He stayed for a week working with the police, meeting with the victims' families, and attending funerals. He ultimately decided that the future profits of the store would go to organizations working for violence prevention and victims' rights.

Howard Schultz "gets it." A common quote of the Starbucks team tells it all:

"We aren't in the coffee business serving people. We're in the people business serving coffee."

EXPECT
to WIN

One of my favorite things to do at work is reading letters or e-mail from customers who share their stories about how our products have made a positive difference in their lives, or in their business. It makes me feel great.

Not long ago I got a letter from Mark Wilkerson, an executive for a major insurance company. One of our gift books inspired Mark to tell a story about how something his **DAD TOLD HIM AS A CHILD HAD SHAPED HIS LIFE.** I'm sharing it with you because I think it's wonderful advice for any leader.

When Mark was growing up he loved baseball and his Dad was the coach of his Little League Baseball team. He remembered his Dad saying repeatedly, prepare for each play and know what to do with the baseball if it is hit to you. Then he said, **"I WANT ALL OF YOU TO WANT THE BALL TO BE HIT TO YOU!"**

His dad said, "Look over your options. Decide what you should do, take a deep breath and let it out, raise up on your toes to be ready, and say to yourself …

HIT THE BALL TO ME!

Then if you make the play, be humble. If you make an error, put it behind you and keep doing the same thing on every pitch."

At the end of Mark's letter he said, "Mr. Anderson, I want to share a poem with you that I wrote when my Dad died in 1988." His poem certainly inspired me, and with Mark's permission, I'm honored to share it with you.

A TRIBUTE
"THANKS DAD"

When our team is in the field,
The other at the plate–
The last half inning to be played,
One play will seal our fate.

Bases are loaded there are two outs,
We've fought to get this far–
The pressure high, adrenaline flowing–
Our record could be marred.

We're ahead by just one run,
It's very close you see–
This is the point where most folks say–
Don't hit the ball to me.

Encouraged and taught to trust myself,
With confidence by Dad –
In opportunity there is no losing,
Just lessons to be had.

So I take a breath and ask myself,
What if it comes my way:
I make the decision to smile and say,
Hit the Ball to me, I can make the play!

That is life in the world today,
Outside the ole ball park,
For the lasting help and faith each play,
Thanks Dad, Love Mark

IN MEMORY OF
EARNEST JEFFERSON WILKERSON
7/7/29-8/9/88

"Quality Is The Mother ...
And We Don't Mess
With Mom."

We embraced this "Quality motto" early on at Successories and I was greatly influenced by my creative partner and friend, Michael McKee. Our paper stock, our color separations, our frames, and even our shipping cartons were of the highest quality. **It was one of our core values.**

I recall an incident in 1988 when we were at about $5 million in sales. Cash was tight and we were watching every penny. Mike brought a copy of a new print into my office. It had just come off the press. **As we were congratulating one another, my assistant walked in and pointed to an apostrophe in the quote at the bottom of the print.** It should have come before the "S" instead of behind the "S." Michael and I sat there stunned, because to reprint it would cost approximately $5,000, which unfortunately we didn't have at the time. Although we both knew that 999 people out of 1,000 wouldn't notice the misplaced apostrophe, our commitment to quality gave us only one choice ... destroy the prints and start over. It was a gut-wrenching decision, given our financial situation, but the right one. **It left no doubt with our team that we were willing to walk the talk when it came to quality.**

"Quality is never
It is always the
intention, sincere
direction, and
It represents the
of many

an accident ...
result of high
 effort, intelligent
skillful execution.
wise choice
alternatives."

— WILL FOSTER

Know the Power of
ONE PAGE

Joe Calhoon and Bruce Jeffrey are consultants who specialize in helping companies create a simple one page strategic plan. I love the idea because there is something magic about one page. Here are the 6 key elements of the plan:

VISION: A clear picture of your destination

MISSION: The driving purpose of your business

VALUES: The guide you use for decision making and how you treat each other

OBJECTIVES: The numbers you track

STRATEGIES: The paths you've decided to take

PRIORITIES: The work that needs to get done and who needs to do it

According to Calhoon and Jeffrey, they've never seen a business plan that was too short, but they have seen hundreds that would make an acceptable cure for insomnia. **They also said that once the management team understands the process, they have never encountered a company that couldn't fit their plan on one page.** Does it take a little more time to "drill down?" Sure it does, but it's well worth it because it forces you to cut out a lot of verbiage and make decisions on what's most important.

I love the quote from Lincoln when he said, **"I apologize for writing such a long letter, but I didn't have the time to write a short one."**

Take the time. You and your team will be glad you did.

"Focus on
the critical few,
and not the
insignificant
many."

— Anonymous

Even EAGLES
Need a Push

The eagle gently coaxed her offspring toward the edge of the nest. Her heart quivered with conflicting emotions as she felt their resistance to her persistent nudging. *"Why does the thrill of soaring have to begin with the fear of falling?"* she thought. This ageless question still remained unanswered for her.

As in the tradition of the species, her nest was located high upon the shelf of a sheer rock face. Below there was nothing but air to support the wings of each child. *"Is it possible that this time it will not work?"* she thought. Despite her fears, the eagle knew it was time. Her parental mission was all but complete. There remained one final task **– the push.**

The eagle drew courage from an innate wisdom. Until her children discovered their wings, there was no purpose for their lives. Until they learned how to soar, they would fail to understand the privilege of having been born an eagle. *The push was the greatest gift she had to offer.* It was her supreme act of love. And so, one by one, she pushed them and they flew.

My friend, David McNally, wrote these words in his book, *Even Eagles Need A Push*. It's human nature to take the path of least resistance. Although most people truly want to reach their full potential, they don't always have the initiative and the discipline to get started on their own. One of your greatest responsibilities as a leader is to enable your people to be all they can be. Many times "the push," with a little encouragement, is all they need.

Always look for opportunities to challenge your best people because many of them are like sticks of dynamite; the power's on the inside, but nothing happens until the fuse gets lit.

"YOU NEVER KNOW WHEN A MOMENT AND A FEW SINCERE WORDS CAN HAVE AN IMPACT ON A LIFE."

— ZIG ZIGLAR

Burn Brightly Without
Burning Out

Jim Cathart is a friend and a great speaker. To manage your energy, Jim feels you need to find the pace at which you perform best. This is the **"zone"** at which you are most creative, unstressed, happy and productive. He defines the "zones" as follows:

ABOVE THE ZONE: First you experience stress and frustration, then anxiety, and finally burnout. At this level you are overwhelming yourself with too many things to accomplish at one time. Lighten up a bit to get back on track.

IN THE ZONE: You are at your best. Not stressed, going with the flow of work naturally, productive and self-assured, challenged but not overwhelmed, motivated and able to roll with problems.

BELOW THE ZONE: First you experience boredom, then apathy, and finally depression. You feel useless and artificial; self-esteem suffers. Bite off more and take greater challenges to get back on track.

Finally, protecting and replenishing your emotional energy is critical for every leader. Mira Kirshenbaum, in her book *The Emotional Energy Factor,* offers a refreshing, down-to-earth approach:

"First you **plug the leaks**: learn to recognize what drains your energy … life situations, toxic people, or habits such as worry, indecision or guilt. Second, you **identify what fills your tank** – pleasure, solitude, anticipation, or fun – and give yourself more."

"THINGS THAT MATTER MOST MUST NEVER BE AT THE MERCY OF THINGS THAT MATTER LEAST."

— GOETHE

TURN UP THE
Fun-O-Meter

Robin Crow, in his book *Rock Solid Leadership* tells about visiting his sister, Laura, who worked for Southwest Airlines. He said, "When we entered the building, which is home to over 3000 employees, I noticed over the elevator, etched in glass, was Southwest Airlines' mission statement:

"The MISSION of Southwest Airlines is dedication to the HIGHEST QUALITY of *Customer Service* delivered with a Sense of *Warmth*, *Friendliness*, *Individual Pride* and *Company Spirit*."

Nothing too unusual about that, except for the fact it didn't even mention planes. Then, as I walked off the elevator onto the second floor, I was overwhelmed by these endless hallways filled with thousands of pictures. I wish you could have been there. There were photos of employees at charity ballgames, Christmas parties and company picnics. There were letters from celebrities and business competitors. There were articles and clippings about Southwest as well as posters and brochures from the early days when the airline was just getting started."

According to Robin, here's the story ...

"When Southwest Airlines built their headquarters about 15 years ago, they decided to fill their walls with photos of memorabilia. President Colleen Barrett, (known as the "heart" of the company), began the tradition of asking employees to submit their own mementos to represent their personal lives and their experiences at Southwest. **The result is basically an enormous company scrapbook.** I saw a cheerleading uniform, an old flight attendant uniform, and my favorite, a crushed tuba (although it did make me think twice about checking my guitar as luggage) – all matted and framed behind glass. Each picture is a piece of what makes Southwest Airlines one of the most extraordinary companies in the world. These halls went on seemingly forever. Imagine, it's a five story building and those photos are on every level, floor to ceiling. There was one hallway completely devoted to photos of employees and their pets. **It was like the Smithsonian of employee appreciation.** But as I started looking more closely at the photos, I noticed that most of them included at least one picture with Herb Keller, (their CEO), hanging out with that employee at a staff picnic or some other celebration – always laughing and having a great time. It became so obvious to me that Herb's enthusiasm and spirit of celebration is at the core of what Southwest stands for as a company. And let me tell you, at Southwest they know how to celebrate. They know the importance of having fun at work. Laura says that it's not uncommon to see a spontaneous parade marching through headquarters in the middle of a busy workday, or to see a department playing a game of hackey sack in the hallway or testing out their long jump skills. As all this was sinking in, I began to understand why Southwest's mission statement focused on **"Customer Service, Individual Pride and Company Spirit"** over talking about airplanes. Southwest Airlines is all about people serving people."

THE RESULTS
While some of America's mammoth airlines are filing for bankruptcy, Southwest is thriving and in the black. In fact, they are now celebrating 33 consecutive years of profitability and their market value is worth more than the next four airlines combined.

So, one more time …
Turn up your Fun-O-Meter.
Having fun with your team creates a magical bond like nothing else you can do.

The ONE Thing That Changes EVERYTHING

There is one thing that is common to every individual, team, family, organization, nation, economy, and civilization throughout the world — one thing which, if removed, will destroy the most powerful government, the most successful business, the most thriving economy, the most influential leadership, the greatest friendship, the strongest character, the deepest love. On the other hand, if developed and leveraged, that one thing has the potential to create unparalleled success and prosperity in every dimension of life. Yet, it is the least understood, most neglected, and most underestimated possibility of our time.

That one thing is TRUST.

Contrary to what most people believe, trust is not some soft, illusive quality that you either have or you don't; rather trust is a pragmatic, tangible, actionable asset that you can create — much faster than you probably think possible.

While corporate scandals, terrorist threats, office politics, and broken relationships have created low trust on almost every front, I contend that the ability to establish, grow, extend, and restore trust is not only vital to our personal and interpersonal well-being; it is the key leadership competency of the new global economy.

I am also convinced that in every situation,

NOTHING IS AS FAST AS THE SPEED OF TRUST.

And, contrary to the popular belief, trust is something you can do something about. In fact, you can get good at creating it.

These words were written by Stephen M. R. Covey in the introduction of his book titled, *The Speed of Trust*. Like the air we breathe, we too often take this critical intangible for granted. I urge you to read Covey's book … *it helps every leader to truly understand how trust is the foundation for any true and lasting success.*

TRUST MEN and they will be true to you; TREAT THEM GREATLY, and they will show themselves great.

— Ralph Waldo Emerson

KNOW THE POWER OF
HUMILITY

I've lived in Chicago for the past 30 years, and as you might expect, I'm a huge Chicago Bears fan. Over the past few years, I watched one man emerge as the leader of the team. **His name ... Brian Urlacher.** No question, Urlacher is a very talented football player. He's made the Pro Bowl for the last 6 years as a middle linebacker. But, if you're a football fan, you know there are a lot of very talented football players who never become the unquestioned leader of their team.

Why is that? Obviously, there are many reasons a leader can emerge from the pack; but in Urlacher's case,

IT IS HIS HUMILITY AND HIS PASSION FOR THE GAME.

I must say, for a superstar athlete, his humility is beyond refreshing. He never talks about himself, his achievements, his statistics; but, he is always the first to praise and defend his teammates and his coaches. When asked how he wanted to be remembered, he said,

"NUMBER ONE, I WANT TO BE REMEMBERED AS A GREAT TEAMMATE. AS A GUY WHO PLAYED HARD AND LOVED FOOTBALL."

Then he was asked about his success in the NFL. He said, "I think I've adjusted pretty well, thanks to good coaches and great teammates. I won't say that I'm lucky, but just fortunate, I guess … I'm very blessed."

So many times, the difference in a good leader vs. a great leader is one word … HUMILITY. A great leader is never afraid to poke fun at himself, and is always first to give all the due credit to others.

If You Chase Two Rabbits,
Both Will Escape

At Successories in 1997, I learned about the power of focus the hard way. I didn't — and I paid the price. Golf was the hot sport because Tiger Woods had just come on the scene. We decided to purchase a small catalog company called British Links, a leader in golf art and golf gifts. The logic was simple:

1. We understood the specialty catalog business, and were already mailing 20 million catalogs a year.

2. We understood the wall décor/framing business. Successories had become one of the largest framers in the country and half of the British Links' sales were from framed wall décor.

I won't bore you with the details of why this venture flopped, but within three years we sold the golf company for next to nothing. However, the most devastating part of the deal was not the money we lost from the sale of British Links, but the momentum we had lost growing Successories, our core business.

In hindsight, I was an idiot! It was like Ray Kroc saying, after having opened twenty McDonald's, it's time to get into the pizza business. Many other businesses — like Starbucks and FedEx — focused their way to success. Repeat after me,

LESS IS MORE, LESS IS MORE...

"In business, real discipline comes in saying

NO

to the wrong opportunities."

— JIM COLLINS

COMMUNICATE,

COMMUNICATE,

COMMUNICATE

Dr. Karen Otazo in her book, the *Truth About Being a Leader*, says there are **3 KEYS TO EFFECTIVE COMMUNICATION:**

1

WHAT'S HAPPENING ...

Share as much as you can about the company's goals and current projects, especially any good news ... but, also be proactive if things aren't going as planned.

2

WHAT'S COMING UP ...

This is a bit like "coming attractions." Your team is always interested in what's new.

3

HOW THEY'RE DOING ...

This one is critical. Look for opportunities, private and public, to say good things, or talk about how they could do better. Most people want to know how they're doing, but are afraid to ask. It is very important to visit, and connect with team members personally.

The great leader truly understands that effective communication is the key that unlocks the door to trust.

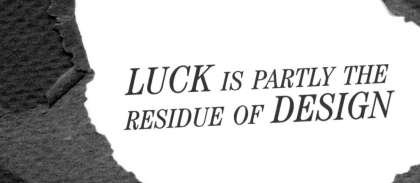

LUCK IS PARTLY THE RESIDUE OF *DESIGN*

Best-selling author, Harry Beckwith, wrote this about luck: "For years in our work, we have preached the value of velocity. *Successful companies succeed because they move, just as the individuals within them move, too.* At first these companies and these people seem lucky. So often they are in the right place at the right time. But they weren't in one place. *They were in several — and one turned out to be right. They realized that luck was out there, and the key was getting into its path.* Not certain which path luck might be on, these people chose several and luck collided with them."

For many years, Darrel Royal was the football coach for the University of Texas. They always had great teams and winning records. Sometimes, however, when they won a close game a sportswriter would suggest that while the Longhorns were skilled they had been lucky on that day. Hearing it one time too often, Coach Royal finally said … *"Luck is partly the residue of design, the simple act of being prepared for luck when it arrives."* And there is something else to luck, Royal said: *Luck follows speed.*

Move and luck finds you. Move quickly and it finds you more often.

"IT'S TEMPTING
WAIT FOR
TO YOU. BUT
IT'S TOO BUSY.
THERE. YOU
GO FOR IT."

TO SIT AND
LIFE TO COME
IT CAN'T,
LIFE IS OUT
HAVE TO

— HARRY BECKWITH

PATIENCE IS BITTER,
BUT THE FRUIT CAN BE SWEET

Leo Tolstoy said, *"The two most powerful warriors are patience and time."*

If I had read that quote 25 years ago, it would have meant little to me. But, today I have a few **"business battle scars"** that could have easily been avoided had I listened to what Tolstoy said.

A few years ago, I had a speaking engagement in Hawaii. I arrived about midnight and a driver met me at the airport to take me to my hotel. He was a young man with a real passion for life. On the way to the hotel, he shared his love for surfing. I asked him if it was dangerous and he said, **"Very dangerous, if you don't know what you're doing."** He said that many people drown when a large wave takes them under and instincts tell them to fight to get back to the surface. The key, he said, is to do just the opposite; let your body go limp and the currents will bring you to the surface. **As a leader there are times to act, and there are times to wait for the right answers to surface.** Remember the quote from a very wise man... Benjamin Franklin,

"He that can have patience can have what he will."

Know the Magic of

Pulling Together

Not long ago, a friend sent me the story of "Old Warwick." It brought a smile to my face, and I think it shares a wonderful lesson for every leader to learn.

A man was lost while driving through the country. As he tried to reach for the map, he accidentally drove off the road into a ditch. Though he wasn't injured, his car was stuck deep in the mud. So the man walked to a nearby farm to ask for help. "Warwick can get you out of that ditch," said the farmer, pointing to an old mule standing in a field. The man looked at the decrepit old mule and looked at the farmer who just stood there repeating,

"Yep, old Warwick can do the job." The man figured he had nothing to lose. The two men and the mule made their way back to the ditch. The farmer hitched the mule to the car. With a snap of the reins he shouted,

"Pull, Fred! Pull, Jack! Pull, Ted! Pull, Warwick!" And the mule pulled that car right out of the ditch.

The man was amazed. He thanked the farmer, patted the mule, and asked, "Why did you call out all of those names before you called Warwick?"

The farmer grinned and said, "Old Warwick is just about blind. As long as he believes he's part of a team, he doesn't mind pulling."

Adapted from *Some Folks Feel the Rain: Others Just Get Wet*, by James W. Moore.

"Teamwork is the ability a common vision. individual organizational objectives. allows common uncommon results.

to work together toward
The ability to direct
accomplishment toward
It is the fuel that
people to obtain

— SUCCESSORIES® PRINT

Recognition is a NEED We all CRAVE

Dr. Abraham Maslow, one of the founders of modern psychology, said this: **"Recognition is a need we all crave, and there are no exceptions."** One of your greatest challenges as a manager is how to help your people fill this need.

Use your imagination for a few seconds. Pretend that you are in a football game. You're in the end zone waiting for the opening kickoff. You see the ball floating through the air and you step up to catch it on the 2 yard line. You head for the middle of the field; you dodge a couple of tacklers; you cut right and head down the sidelines for 98 yards. You reach the end zone, hands in the air. You turn around, and … nothing. Not a sound. Your teammates are just strolling off the field. You think … what happened? Did I run the wrong way? But there are no boos. You think … something feels terribly wrong!

But you know what? … that's how it feels in many homes and workplaces everyday. Somebody does something great and they hear absolutely nothing.

Mario Fernandez said it best … "The Human spirit is nurtured by praise, as much as a seedling is nurtured by the soil, the water, and the sun."

"The greatest
principle in
'The things that
and appreciated

management
the world is
get rewarded
get done'"

— Michael Le Boeuf

Identify your
CORE VALUES

There are two things I believe with all my heart:

(1) Core Values are critical to build great brands and great companies, and

(2) They must be continuously enforced to truly make it a part of your company culture.

Why the need for values in an organization? Core values serve as critical guides for making decisions, and when in doubt, they cut through the fog like a beacon in the night.

Identifying the core values that define your company is one of the more important functions of leadership. They can make or break your long term success. But, you also should know that gaps between your values and your actions can do more harm than good. In other words, if you talk about building a customer-first culture, but fail to do so … you'll lose the respect of your employees and your customers.

Therefore, as a leader, you must select your core values carefully because once you commit, your credibility is on the line.

"**GOALS** are for the future;
GOALS are set;
GOALS change;
you can count on."

VALUES are for now.
VALUES are lived.
VALUES are rocks that

— SHELDON BOWLES

WALK YOUR TALK

A few years ago I was invited to spend some time with Ken Blanchard at his lake home in upstate New York. Over the last 20 years Ken has probably sold more books than any other business author. His classic, *The One Minute Manager*, has sold over 10 million copies. He has also built a large training company with the focus on **servant leadership** and **customer service**.

I've had the good fortune to meet many successful businessmen, authors, and speakers during my career, but, I've never met anyone that "walked the talk" more than Ken. He gets it. The first night of my visit to Ken's lake home, we were sitting on the deck with Humberto, his son-in-law, talking about some ways we could work together. It was about 10 p.m., when all of a sudden Ken jumped up and asked to be excused. He returned about 10:20 and Humberto asked … "What happened?" Ken said,

"I can't believe it; I forgot to call Dorothy on her birthday."

Later that night, after Ken had gone to bed, Humberto told me that Dorothy is an 85 year old part time employee for the company. It then dawned on me that at 10 p.m. Ken left to spend almost 20 minutes talking to Dorothy and inquiring about how she had spent her special day. **However, after spending more time with Ken over the next year, I came to realize that this was no fluke. This is who he is.** The last time while visiting him at his San Diego office, I learned that one of his employees who worked in the warehouse had recently passed away. On that day, Ken had invited the employee's wife to come to his office. When she arrived, he spent an hour walking around with her carrying a tape recorder to record all of the wonderful memories that other employees had of her husband. When the wife left she said it was a day she'd never forget.

You see, what many leaders would have considered a waste of time, Ken saw it as an opportunity to serve and to thank his people. He doesn't do it because it's expected of him, he does it because he truly cares. It comes from his heart, and his people love him for being the servant leader that he is.

This is an **old Chinese poem** that offers wonderful advice for any leader:

GO *to the people*
LIVE *among the people*
LEARN *from them*
LOVE *them.*
START *with what they know,*
BUILD *on what they have.*
But of the **BEST** *leaders,*
When their **TASK** *is accomplished,*
Their **WORK** *is done,*
The **PEOPLE** *will remark,*
"WE HAVE DONE IT OURSELVES."

ABOUT THE AUTHOR

MAC ANDERSON is the founder of Simple Truths and Successories, Inc., the leader in designing and marketing products for motivation and recognition. These companies, however, are not the first success stories for Mac. He was also the founder and CEO of McCord Travel, the largest travel company in the Midwest, and part owner/VP of sales and marketing for Orval Kent Food Company, the country's largest manufacturer of prepared salads.

His accomplishments in these unrelated industries provide some insight into his passion and leadership skills. He also brings the same passion to his speaking where he speaks to many corporate audiences on a variety of topics, including leadership, motivation, and team building.

Mac has authored or co-authored eighteen books that have sold over three million copies. His titles include:

- *Change is Good … You Go First*
- *Charging the Human Battery*
- *Customer Love*
- *Finding Joy*
- *Learning to Dance in the Rain*
- *212°: The Extra Degree*
- *212° Service*
- *Motivational Quotes*
- *One Choice*

- *The Nature of Success*
- *The Power of Attitude*
- *The Power of Kindness*
- *The Essence of Leadership*
- *The Road to Happiness*
- *The Dash*
- *To a Child, Love is Spelled T-I-M-E*
- *You Can't Send a Duck to Eagle School*
- *What's the Big Idea?*

For more information about Mac, *visit www.simpletruths.com*